PROEMS
&POEMS

WSU Press Art Series

RUTH SLONIM

PROEMS & POEMS

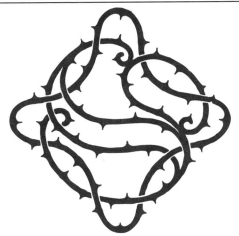

Washington State University Press
Pullman, Washington

Washington State University Press, Pullman, Washington 99164-5910

©1992 by the Board of Regents of Washington State University
All rights reserved
First Printing 1992

Library of Congress Cataloging-in-Publication Data
Slonim, Ruth.
   Ruth Slonim—proems and poems / Ruth Slonim.
      p. cm.—(WSU Press art series)
   ISBN 0-87422-084-X (hd.).—ISBN 0-87422-077-7 (pbk.)
   I. Title.   II. Series.
PS3537.L67R88 1992   91-42039
811'.54—dc20   CIP
                                                                   Rev.

To Pervasive Peace

Table of Contents

In Transit

Acknowledgments

Some poems in this volume have previously appeared in:

Botteghe Oscure, XXI (Rome), 1958

Deep Down Things: Poems of the Inland Pacific Northwest, ed. by Ron McFarland, Franz Schneider, and Kornel Skovajsa (Pullman: Washington State University Press, 1990)

International Who's Who in Poetry Anthology (Cambridge: Melrose Press, 1972)

Outer Traces/Inner Places: Selected Poems by Ruth Slonim (Washington, D. C.: Three Continents Press, 1981)

San Francisco: "The City" in Verse (Pullman: Washington State University Press, 1965)

Washington State Review, Spring 1960

Genesis

Whenever someone has inquired as to what prompted me to write poetry, my smiling response has been "a congenital condition." This condition has persisted since my first poem was written in early childhood. The more difficult question is regarding the nature of the creative processes by which a poem comes into being. As Leonard Bacon tells us, in reviewing Melville Cane's *The Making of a Poem,*

> ...it's no picnic to explain
> How poems breed between the heart and brain,
> How sacred idiocy or sacred rage
> May end as verses written on a page.
> However vigorous or slight the urge,
> Still from the same Unconscious they
> emerge.

Later in Mr. Bacon's discourse, he queries and then responds:

> How does a poem come then?...
> Only, I say, "by cock-eyed miracle"
> At point where parallel joins parallel,
> By solution of equations whose quaint roots
> Grow into trees that yield surprising fruits.

Small wonder that the poetic process tends to elude description!

One might ask whether the writing of poetry is more rational than intuitive. In my experience, the initial creation of a poem is predominantly intuitive; the essential refining of a poem, more rational. I do not exclude the reason or the intuition from either imperative and indeed regard both the initial expression and the polishing thereafter as part of *one* process. On occasion, no need exists to alter a single image; no wisps of language require snipping. More frequently, however, even a very brief poem invites the most intense scrutiny and possible revision. One gropes for *le mot juste,* the exactly right word; the most satisfactory reinforcement of meaning and sensibility, usually via figurative implicitness and resonant language. My especially memorable recollection of the British Museum in London is of the manuscripts of John Keats, that feverish poetic genius fighting a losing battle against time and his physical debility. Snuffed out in his mid-twenties and poignantly knowing that his candle burned low, he nevertheless took time to revise and revise and again revise all those poems that to this day gleam on the page. In examining his manuscripts, one confronted line after line and word after word crossed out. William Butler Yeats was similarly disposed to revision, claiming late in his life that there were perhaps only four poems that he had not felt compelled to alter. The poet-anthologist Louis Untermeyer may have hit on the secret of all creative excellence when he expressed in a poem the wish that he be kept "yet unsatisfied." It seems to me that no artist, whatever his or her medium, would dare be too readily or easily sanguine. This is at once a stimulating and intimidating requisite that profoundly equates integrity with responsible creativity.

Some years ago Amy Lowell aptly defined a poet as an individual having an "extraordinarily sensitive and active subconscious personality, fed by and feeding a non-resistant consciousness." Sometimes the feeding process is of long duration; at other times, relatively brief. There are instances when it is possible to isolate and identify the external stimulus which has produced a poem. More often the consciousness contains "no record of the initial impulse." Words have a way of arriving in full dress, demanding immediate hospitality though often having provided no forewarning.

I do not write because I should but because I must and not primarily for public consumption. I do not choose any subjects or forms to accord with prevailing or traditional attitudes, modish or antiquated stylistic tendencies, nor do I decry the effectiveness of other modes and other pens. Momentarily taking liberty with Descartes, "I am; therefore I write." What I write may be far from perfect. Its qualitative validity must emanate from the integrity of invention and attention. Poems are bred of diverse realities, elusive intangibles, and the distillation of cumulative and immediate experience, one would hope implying some measure of accrued illumination and inspiration.

By now you are no doubt well aware that

    . . . it's no picnic to explain
    How poems breed between the heart and brain.

Perhaps, like Lord Byron when reacting to Coleridge's "explaining metaphysics to the nation," you wish I would "explain [my] explanation."

PANTHEON

In this mini-Pantheon are a random few of the many persons whose creative capabilities have led to exemplary and memorable bequests.

Emily Dickinson

Miss Emily, so physically small,
imaginatively ultra tall,
retreated from the press and scurry
of an intimidating world.
Within her embracing Amherst home,
secure from vulnerability,
she read a universal scene.
For Emily-sized poems she would glean
      love, death, and immortality
      the declamations of a bee
        nutritious matter
served on her own ingenious platter.

Jonathan Swift
(St. Patrick's Cathedral)

In the Cathedral-quiet of this hour
Dean Swift remains a presence here
centuries beyond his temporal power.
Abrasive though he was and damned as misanthrope,
Jonathan Swift made cause with those most
                            needing hope.
To Dublin's suffering poor and mentally afflicted
            he opened purse and door,
and later was convicted for this sharing
when sentenced to his own demented bearing.

Claude Monet

This French artist lit the sun.
Absorbed with light and atmospheric
          variations,
Impressionist Monet left gifts of
          grain stacks,
bridges, Rouen Cathedral in successive
          versions,
          and much else—
evocative testaments in paint that hang now
          in one's cranial gallery.
Swirl and parallel, subtle glow
          still resonate
          to prod remembrance
of innovative Claude Monet
having his forever-luminous say.

Feodor M. Dostoevski

Tutored by personal tragedy,
a life of pitch-and-toss,
    of crucial loss,
his prison stint and frequent seizures
        added to intensity.
With a fictional eye on the human psyche
and on intricate moral cancers,
this novelistic spy implied
simplistic and complex answers.

James Joyce

The black-eel Liffey thrusts its length
            astride a Dublin day.
Splotched curbstones indiscreetly tell
night secrets syllabled in smell.
Some gone astray, now pray;
some pray to go astray—
anemic lives needing transfusion.

Here rebel genius walked the crack
in ramparts that were frail,
chafed at a less-than-emerald path,
choosing to set sail.
Escaping every ritual bond,
bold dreams embarked for earthier ground
than native soil assured.

In the beginning was the word
foretelling Bloomsday end;
Dubliners devoutly doubt
their ex-officio friend.

Martin Luther King, Jr.

Sharing your compassionate dream
      yet unfulfilled,
despite mean impulses of some to growl,
      not smile,
      smiling is my style;
its opposite dismembers dreams.

I envision bombs transformed to trowels,
distrust long past recall,
the world a gracious neighborhood
made comfortable for all.

Jane Austen
(Winchester Cathedral, England)

No mention here of books
or an immortal pen.
Who loved her
knew her loving
and told that truth of bone.
With unpretentious caring
they claimed her as their own.

Franz Kafka

Your fire blazed for a while
and then with strength and style
            you took your leave
not planning that one grieve,
not willing words to still remind,
to make a moment's stir or prod
            the blind.
That which you were, you were.

Unsung you chose to go
but we have seen and know
how arduously you moved on paths
            of fright
from unremitting darkness
that dissembles wrong and right.

Ezra Pound

A leaning tower of Pisa,
his canto-by-canto slant
divulged misbegotten haunts,
argument by rant.
Self-consciously erudite,
in broadcasts and on paper
he paid with intellectual blight
for flagrant verbal capers.

Mastery of poetics was an Ezra plus;
so too, the astute critical flair
keeping top-notch pens in good repair.
Young poets got their helpful share.

Escaping treason's blunt finale,
shed of a catatonic state,
about to arrive at journey's end
he understood too late.

William Butler Yeats

I
(St. Stephens Green, Dublin)

There he stands
looking more William than Willie.
In Henry Moore's compassionate hands
stature removes the aloof pout,
the anarchic lock of hair;
transcends the cumulative doubt
that worth is everywhere.
Metallic subtleties guard human secrets well,
distill in stylized height
what lesser skill might tell.
This sculpted poem in run-on lines
hails Dublin's hoi polloi;
children playing games
hide behind a mammoth toy
to feel themselves the giant,
if only for an instant.
Men walk home from their pint
and keep their distance.

II
(Drumcliff, County Sligo)

'Horseman, pass by'
and know that I, W. B. Yeats,
lie here interred.
A cryptic posture is my final word.
Mists that becloud my Sligo sleep
make better shroud than critic-notions.
Theory and grumble, voiced devotions,
unwrite the light.
Though mountains crumble
none shall know
whence I came to where I go.

Sinclair Lewis

(first U. S. Nobel Laureate in Literature)

A once-lanky lad from a Midwest town
invented its literary counterpart.
Gopher Prairie claimed Main Street, USA
and a gung ho businessman named Babbitt—
grist for the author's satirical habit.
Hitting his stride in the 1920's,
later books less taut and firm
still contained the critical germ.

After losing a son in World War II
some of Red Lewis's starch ran out;
yet he journeyed on with wide-open eyes,
cutting bigotry and hypocrisy down to size.

Gabriel Fielding
(Alan Barnsley)

As raconteur and thespian
you chose your on-stage roles,
gifts of pride and vibrancy
on a pyrotechnic spree
being bought and sold.

Connoisseur of nature's spread—
fresh-water challenges, rocky
               ledge,
trees and birds to paint or ponder
filled you with a deeper wonder.

Removed from your tumultuous self,
surrounded by familial love
and in communion with your God,
you listened to an ethereal voice
confirming the mystery of choice.
As poet-mystic you would unload
all obstacles to the ultimate road.

G. B. S.
(Bernard Shaw)

Two decades past his Dublin birth
      a red and ready head
took leave of personal weather
        marred by storm
to set his course for London latitudes;
there brisker exercise would keep him warm
and nourishment derive from Fabian foods.
Leaving Irish fantasy behind
his luggage carried other gifts of mind,
the teasing blasphemy and ethical thrust
that pulverize pretension; sift its dust.
From 'Celtic Twilight' came dramatic day,
Shavian salvos cracking feet of clay.

Arthur Rimbaud

Cocks crow the seminal day;
reveille sounds far away in orange hells.

Shivering on hot coals of why,
we live our nascent days
those wide-eyed days we die.

Mahalia Jackson
(Berkeley, CA concert)

Swollen with music
a mammoth in ice-blue evening gown
and bedroom slippers
worn on heroically supportive feet,
gave gifts of soul
with every syllable of sound.
Transcendent resonance outreached
the monotonal ground.

Sean O'Casey

Envoy from a sour slum,
your voice rings true to
those unkind and kind.
In Dublinese you spoke
as partisan of decencies.
Put off by shibboleth,
bestirred by paradox,
you picked encrusted locks,
then threw away old keys.

F. Scott Fitzgerald

Riches unpawnable with pride
he pawned to buy a larger scope;
inward-lurking, quick to hide,
the poor man drank his pint of hope.
He drank it to the final dregs,
then dipped his pen in empty kegs.

George Washington Carver

Eventual significance was promised by his name
derived from past distinction that led to
      present fame.
Diminutive in stature, Dr. Carver broke new ground
      for creative agriculture.
His discoveries would redound to industry, nutrition,
      and more productive soil;
      sweet potatoes, peanuts, soy beans
        giving focus to his toil.

James Thurber

Ultimately blind,
he saw to draw
in words or graphic lines
the laugh and pang of recognition.
With wit and poignancy
his keen internal vision
has helped the sighted see.

Helen Keller

Annie Sullivan, an inspiring teacher,
spurred an intrepid spirit.
Blind, deaf and mute Helen Keller
          found her voice.
With persistence and poise she learned
          to speak.
Articulate grace outwitted defeat.

Wolfgang Amadeus Mozart

Genius bequeathed a repertoire
so vibrantly phenomenal
so seemingly inevitable
one wonders what sustained
that flow of inspiration
that intactness of creation—
genius inexplainable and unexplained.

Was self-doubt or ego attendant
            at that birth
        of extraordinary music,
          its quintessential worth?

Eleanor Roosevelt

In high pitched somewhat crackly voice
A First Lady of humanity inscribed
the Universal Declaration of Human Rights.
She lived what she professed
and by example urged that none transgress
against those who differ in aspect or in view.
Choosing to animate those verities that overtake
hurtful distrust and defiling hate,
a towering presence epitomized what yet remains
unrealized.
Hospitable to diversity, she opted for cordiality
that some prefer to shun, even as they devoutly
pray
"Thy will be done."

R. Buckminster Fuller
(Imagician)

A native gift of crossed eyes
helped you realize;
freed you from stricture,
from every list of "is" and "isn't"
that manacles "might be."
You see configurations
in your teeming head
and on the teeming sphere called
                    Earth,
the synergy in every quirk and
                    miracle of mind
that binds with love.
You populate our spaceship planet
with insights born of eyesight
                    gone askew.
You are unique design come true.

Atoms assembled in the brain
are made "Exhibit A" in your display
of engineered felicity.
Your domes now house our history.

Land mass and three-fourths sea
become a humanscape.
Countering entropy and indecision
you speak the poetry of vision
in vocal images of shape.

Martha Graham

Cartographer of modern dance,
you wrought and taught the ways
that merged the dancer and the dance,
setting both ablaze.
Intrinsic taste, a prime resource;
integrity your core,
you called upon your own life-force
    to venture ever more.

Richard Hugo

Robustly genuine,
minus all verbal swagger,
Dick exchanged a Cascade Range
for neighboring Rockies,
casting an inner light
on variable terrain—
glacial lows and fever-inducing
        heights.

Between the sun and moon
his skein unwound too soon.

Darius Milhaud

(. . ."artist and citizen of the world
par excellence") UC, Berkeley

Your home, the world
plants fragile flowers at its door.
Bruised by boisterous winds,
uprooted by the score and millions more,
        their seed remains.
Topographies of loss breed subtle gains.

Haunted by brutalities too profane for grief,
you answered grim largesse with the harmonic
        crest
      of your belief.

Louise Bogan

In sturdy brogans and suit of tweed
this poet-critic stood twice tall.
Her *New Yorker* critiques traversed
those quirks and fathomings
in hobbled lives and lines that sing.
This artist's stirring poetry,
divested of fluff and stratagem,
bespeaks an insightful stance and prowess
wise to the fact that more may be less.

Wilbur and Orville Wright

Daedalus and Icarus imagined flying high;
the sun, a mythic adversary,
nudged an intruder from the sky.
Leonardo da Vinci, conceiving human flight,
spent time and mind designing
a winged bird that might be right.
Not put to the crucial test,
it took the Wright brothers' insight
        to venture a two-step.
They conceived their novel version,
then proved it safe to soar.
This engineered conversion would eventually
                    induce
yet another miracle—Howard Hughes aboard
                a goose!

Theodore Roethke

One moment child; another, ancient's voice;
misery untuned to choice,
you walked a shell-strewn beach where echoes
    roar.
Your heron-words instruct that shore
where mewing gulls retell brave flights.

Plummeting from vapid heights,
you sang the buxom truths of earth;
you danced a waltz for all its worth,
to celebrate in cadenced clue
the dark cacophony of you.

What set swirls in tides of me
you cast adrift on restive sea.

     * * *

   In a dark time,
   shadow to light
   he ventured sight.
   A cratered moon
   coming to fullness
   waned too soon.

     * * *

   Eerie yelps of self
   or self denied
   drown in a scene
   where flotsams mean
   and meanings hide.

   Fluencies abide.

Andrei Sakharov

Knowing travail sharp-edged as tundra winter,
        suffering history's dark gnaw,
this modern Atlas ate his sour bread.
Swallowing raw chunks of reprimand
he kept his head and held truth's scrawny hand.

Marcel Proust

Remembrance of things past
prompts me to have a cup of tea
          with madeleines
while thinking of now and then.

IN TRANSIT

Side-Trip

Crossing the street from somewhere far
I tripped over a morning star;
stood on my head for a thought or two,
then set my feet on the street anew.

In Transit

A pilgrim-child, grown up,
listens to wind-strummed concertizing
                wires,
finds warmth at incremental fires.
Kindled by centuries, a resonant grownup
distills those humbling vibrancies
to fill this day's receptive cup.

Scope

Natives imprinted long-ago topography
where tribal intuitions reverenced land and sea
          and sky,
where wandering and wondering, some prematurely heard
          the owl's foreboding cry.
Pictographs on rock outcroppings,
place names—their singular music to the ear—
memorialize intrepid ones whose measured lives,
bent by climatic onslaughts and the tyranny of fear,
honored their Great Spirit and nature's benefactions.

Elephant-herd hills with wrinkled gray backs,
curvacious softer assertions from the fertile earth
          promised futurity and worth.

Palouse, Enumclaw, Cle Elum, Klickitat, Skamania
Washtucna, Chewelah, Nespelem, Nisqually
Skykomish, Kamloops, Wallula, Walla Walla
          Olalla

Igneous earth and verge of sea nourished intrinsic
          dignity.
Early-comers studied white-capped mountain peaks,
their stunning angularity and awesome gist—
subtle messages in snow and mist;
tall timber scenting western days and nights,
a stalwart river prattling oceanward,
salmon en route to spawning site,
desert sage and plumaged bird.

          Variables of prime terrain,
          encampments on predestined pain.

          Alki
          (by and by)

Derivatives from elsewhere roots
enticed by visionary impulse, hunger, restlessness
brought cargos of diversity by ship and wagon
to this north corner of the West.

Homesteaders staked their claims.
Some planted, some despoiled with gusto and few qualms.
With holier-than-thou disdain for native mores
proficiently these staunch arrivals stood their ground.
Newcomers with alienating zeal would soon find
              belligerence answering in kind.

Yet to be healed, indignities that linger in our midst;
indifference a menacing clenched fist.

From every continent they came,
from all directions in the nation,
westbound Lewis and Clark and long cross-country trains
huffed and puffed by early trail and later rail
leading to cranberry bogs and promissory grain.
A mid-state desert would turn fruitful, thanks
              to irrigation.

  Nisei displacement belatedly redressed
  Creation of Grand Coulee Dam
  A Narrows Bridge collapse
  Mt. St. Helens' molten bombast
     intercepting a jet stream
  Unrehearsed responses to still-persisting
                    ash
  The advent of atomic bombs and Hanford's
              hush-hush scene

  All this high drama and much more
  seeds our after as before.

Changed by a hundred evergreen years, once-wagon tracks
                 now freeways.
Propelled by new technology, metallic bird and satellite
                 take flight;
hurtling through space, their far-flung circuitry
              connects the human race.

Peaceful intentions form and change,
exploring a range one could not know
              a century ago.

Quarry

Seeing a graceful bird in flight
"I" bagged it with unbridled might
and mindless gluttony.
Then blind ego, standing tall,
kicked it to a final fall,
a last indignity.
A bird is merely bird, thought "I"
looking this time at empty sky.

Myopics Anonymous

There go some skittish ones
who choose to be
remote from mutuality.
Wearing themselves so tightly
perhaps they feel the pinch
that bending even slightly
might liberate an inch.

Aspects
(Puerto Rico)

Volatile ones on the street
scan blue-quiet folds in the hills.

Blue-quiet ones on the street
scan volatile folds in the hills.

* * *

Bamboo forests have a rocking chair
creak
when they speak.
Bamboo forests are in graceful repose
when they doze.

* * *

Silver-purple paradox,
beauty, bittersweet,
measured out in tall cane
stalks
for someone else to eat.

Vibrant fields of yes and no
kindle dreams that come
and go.

Desert Flowers

Nubs of cactus prickle into bloom.
Day blossoms too, red-orange
and heavy.
Heavy the decimated fruit
hanging in memory
and in prospect.
Hotter than heat of desert
this mushroom-burst of flower,
this tainted hour.

String Quartet

Synchronized miracles
tell much, not all,
with every rise and fall
        of bow,
each toss of self
(collective selfhood,
reaper of tones to sow).
While you play
deaf Beethoven still hears;
you say his piece for him
these many years beyond
the last quartets
conceived with pain's notation,
            yet serene.
As listeners take their station
for an interlude,
and phrasings mean,
taste bends in attitude
toward whom you now befriend
        by caring.
To reassert a vibrant daring
of mind and heart,
frail strings bind random lives
so often worlds apart.

Scourge

Years ago the scourge of polio
felled those en route to their tomorrow.
Some lost their valiant fight
that brought them to eternal night.
Countering epidemic sorrow
research produced benign vaccines
to intervene against yet more affliction.

Today the scourge is drug addiction,
        a complex social ill
gnawing at inner will that cannot cope.
Leading from bad to worse is tragedy
        and curse.

Why?

Huge tree trunks reduced to stumps
    menace the atmosphere;
hint at the amplitude of earth
depleted of its fruitful worth.
Oceanic depths and tidal sigh
    offer their outcry.
Crucial crops less surely flourish
though tended by green thumbs or
    blithely wild.
Smog and acid rain discourage
sweet prospects for tomorrow's child.
Slaughtering animated trees
    multiplies indignities.
Year after year vulnerable species
    disappear.

    Why, oh why?

As yet protected by the ozone layer
crass indifference dares to leave
its calling-card stain on land and sea,
    scarring human destiny.

    Our poignant cry:
    Why, oh why?

This day's arboreal reply
(a memo to futurity)
affirms centennial burgeoning,
its peaceful-dreamful progeny.
Nurturing planetary health
nurtures the human spirit,
enlarging one's identity
with all who claim this planet.

    Taking heed,
a hundred planted trees are litany
for one day's planting of one seed.

Countables and Unaccountables
(centennial musings)

Millennia are countable
by breaths drawn and expired,
by centuries of plus and minus,
        poignancies afire.
Vision prods the future
through a magnifying past
detailing lost and found,
fertilities and infertilities of ground,
undertows of swollen pride,
games of seek and hide.
On ego-trips some lose their way
quantifying night and day.
More modest venturers discover
eloquence in humble folk
who occasion sweet surprise
sharing sensibility,
widening dull eyes.
Ready warmth and inner spark
illuminate the enigmatic dark.

Easy come easy go insights,
blaring violence in televised fare
disorient innocent travelers
heading for music unheard.
Where, oh where, is that mythical bird?

Hope, thought to be blind, is eternally
                young,
nurturing dreamers and dreams.
Blind strategy with a heavier foot
concocts Machiavellian schemes.
Purveyors of "image" buy and sell
castles of sand in a golden clime,
exacting exorbitant price,
devaluing essence as nickel-and-dime.

"All aboard for the next
            Shangri-La,
the next ingenious wizard
devising the next Hurrah!"

Gardens of knowledge make welcome
those who would eagerly grow
as the recurring spring flowers
            emerging from snow.
Countering distrust and malignant terror
compassionate earthlings score war
            the ultimate error.

From their present-tense perch
viewers attend a play in one act.
What of the fluent continuum,
mystery flowing before and thereafter?
Where the empathic tears
and all-embracing laughter
to groom earth's disheveled family
            far-flung and diverse
for the next centennial chapter?

An American in Dublin

Phoenix Park

Children twitter toward me,
brogued and winged,
their smiling curiosity
        greeting mine.
They titter their delight
at unfamiliar sound,
form rings of radiance
around my Phoenix perch.
Often in duplicate or threes
these innocent fledglings
bend the knees of logic.
Thus renewed, I flutter with
this winged and winning brood.

Bird Feeder

A down-at-the-heels fellow
striding ahead of me
put his hand into a pocket,
went on a lavish spree.
Bread-crumbs were his philanthropy.

Sunday Scene
(Oxford)

Cars whir and whiz
 along this Woodstock Road
as though determined to escape a past
that may outlast capricious wheel and
            petrol-hungry roar.
Appetite for more of now need not refute
those other truths implanted deep.
Where ancient spires still soar,
            old verities will keep
            and yet entice the new
with random scrap and sturdier slice
            of doubts on which to chew.

Wren Library

(Trinity College, Cambridge University)

Christopher Wren wrought miracles
outwitting time;
his was a legacy of light.
Manuscripts in early print,
those of later date
generate brave purposes
of pulse and pen
that say amen to luminous
vision.

Perhaps an architect of new designs
is at this moment borrowing lines
from Trinity
and from a cosmic cue
that promises infinity
another finite view.

Mementos

I hear cries in the stone of an ugly tower.
Where courtyard ravens make raucous pleas
           for food and more food
monarchic whims fed on beheading the innocent
while regal caprice held sway.

I hear moans in unseen Auschwitz ash.
Where goose steps pressed hard toward
           ironclad ovens
         pain left its eternal stain.

I hear boat-people weeping their salt
           in a sea
where capsized intentions drown to be free.

Paying small toll from day to bland day,
I dare not erase those ghosts from my clay.

Bigot

To rationalize stagnation
you eat the poison crumbs
of self-conceived damnation,
then lick your several thumbs.

Exemplar

(Elie Wiesel)

Intellect and empathy
invite enlarged identity.
An offspring of history's
        bestial night
turns on a universal light.

Nature Note

Once upon a once there were
flocks of well-feathered birds
perched atop their wisdom
    staring unblinkingly.
With reputations quite secure
(although the world was mostly blur)
these birds looked wise unthinkingly.

Mock Epic

Through a murky looking-glass
Tweedledum and Tweedledee
mistake each other for the world.
With chronic insularity
they stub their stubborn toes
      on grains of sand,
then curse a bumptious land.
Scoring Humpty Dumpty
because he plainly fell,
they cut themselves in transit
on bits of broken shell.
Oh well, ---

Expediency

Testing the wind for every clue,
jabbering testaments of self
      blocks the spacious
          view.
Frail mortals, panting to get somewhere,
misread mirage-horizons;
pay their respects to vapid gods
      answering in kind;
        calculate odds.
Blind, they grope toward a searing sun
till day is irreversibly done.

Springtide

(1977)

Browning first urged me
to the spring of England,
to cuckoo-refrain
and bluebell-quilted field.
Antiquity and present yield
in fragile balance
speak to my eye and marrow;
this untranslatable lingo
helps me feel the eternality
of gentle things,
the mystery in wings.
Enigmatic steel, fluent oil
becloud these springtime
blossomings of scent and sense.
Nureyev dances in a Festival setting,
Jubilee salvos celebrate the Queen
to tunes of economic fretting,
of resurrecting what has been.
Plus-and-minus poignancies remind
that what is now
contains what lies behind.

Glimpses (from *San Francisco*)

Fishermen's Wharf

Lifting anchor, a sturdy fleet
moves from the Wharf
toward crab-red dawn.
Mindless with sleep,
The City begins its awakening
    yawn.

Cable Clatter

Sounds served up on a pavement-platter.

San Francisco Jazz

San Francisco's two-beat style
traveled many a wistful mile
from New Orleans of the Twenties.
With thump and tuba-razzmatazz
old hands make banjos stutter jazz.
Since early in the Forties
'Kid' Ory's saints have gone marching in
  with trombone-stride;
Lu Watters' trumpet shattered din
in Clubs where echoes hide.
Earl Fatha Hines makes the ivories talk
as spry nostalgia takes its all-night
    walk.

Bouquet

"How about a bunch of violets, Ma'am?
Mighty nice morning. Hope the fog holds off" . . .
and then the cough,
proffered with purple scent.
Coughing again, he smiled,
while I, less valiant,
bought fields of early spring
to ease the sting.

Lost and Found

Descending depth on depth into yourself
you lose your wingward way,
then struggle up through fragile shell
to feed on fresh dismay.
Molting feather-words, you sing;
voluptuous clouds recite
the trenchant litanies of spring,
another plunge from light.

Your broken song, still palpitant,
swells every spring-born bough
with poignant notes that sweetly haunt
the tenuous after-glow.

Once more in ruffled tracks of fright
wings beat against the breast of night,
            abrasive quest.
I reach beyond eclipsing moons
to set torn wings at rest.

Verity

This day is bloom
cherry — plum — almond — peach
      profusions
contradicting magnolia-voiced attitudes
      more staunchly held.
Delicately, in blossom-whispers,
truth titters a few white lies
      that fall in petals.
Only the wise green earth may ever know
fertilities these petals sow.

Pacifica

Always the shore, there to receive
    tide and tide-riding birds
    come from long since . . .
a shifting coast where kelp and clam
      have entity,
where gulls are guest and host.
In rhythms of oceanic surge
Orient and Occident converge.

Vistas

Indifferent cranial weather obscures Mt. Everest
                    and lesser peak
remote from miniscule domains,
provincial habitats of mind
often so meagerly designed
that neither vagrant warmth nor random spark
ignites the obstinate dark.
Still on we climb toward vistas,
indigenous palisade and distant glade;
Leonardo's many voices,
mystifying computer-tongues;
infant gurglings, valedictory speeches,
orbital sounding of far reaches—
                    from ABC to RNA,
an awesome span of fluencies
amending categorical scenes
and lilliputian means.

Tasting the tang in alien realms,
not least ourselves,
commandeers new helms of faith and fire
beyond the local pond and town
where fish in the swim may unwittingly drown.
Reading a cosmic braille makes day of night,
transmuting ignorance to light,
freeing both mind and spirit
from every self-constricting jail.
          Some see but do not see
          companionable diversity.

Hazarding unfamiliar galaxies
and possible avalanche,
essential high-rise rent
for intimations of tomorrow,
the courageous muster strength
to reach toward genuine stars
in illusory skies;
to reach toward being wise.

Yet more vistas pose the way
for robust stride or feet of clay.
Astringent weather points an onward thrust
guided by lineaments of love,
the animating throb and glow
illuminating yes and no.
Integrity informs and warms our quest.
We venture hand in hand in hand
through an intricate learning-land
to welcome syntheses,
the quickening breeze of change,
ennobling constancies —
an infinite range.

Across a slate-gray autumnal sky
migrant Canada geese in flight
honk salvos to a whistling wind
and to impending night.
At home in transit between then and soon
some inner compass clarifies
resonances of space and size
this waning afternoon.

Genesis

Rain speaks no word,
yet is heard.
Snow tells the ground
what seeds expound—
a primordial knowing
that every winged bird
descends to soar;
every after harbors a before.